Arias of A Deaf Mute

By: Chendel Hooks

Art inspired by Leroy White *(www.leroywhiteartworks.com)*

Printed in the United States of America by Apocalypse Publishing LLC

ISBN-978-0-692-07409-1

Preface

I heard their voices speak. Like murmurs from a sunken vessel, barely audible beyond a whisper. I felt their vibrations ripple through me and in that instant, I began to record these last seconds of life. To offer proof, so that we could remember.

Vivid illustrations of tales so broken. An evocative drama that extorts your compassion but spurs the imagination. Like echoes with a heartbeat they reflect from the surface of the page to the core of your consciousness.

As the lights dim and the curtain rises, let go and dream for just a minute. Hear what your eyes see and exhaust any natural limit. These stories contain both their strength and their sorrow. Be here with them now, because they never had tomorrow.

This book is dedicated in loving memory to

Annie Rose Fletcher-James

and

Bettie Beal

Table Of Contents:

Chapter 1: The Die Is Cast

Chapter 2: Breathe

Chapter 3: Incarcerated Introspective

Chapter 4: I DO

Chapter 5: Brazen Wolves

Chapter 6: Seeds Of Malevolence

Chapter 7: Full Disclosure

Chapter 1
THE DIE IS CAST

LES DÉS SONT JETÉS

模具是鑄造的

ويلقى بموت

ЖРЕБИЙ БРОШЕН

LA SUERTE ESTÁ ECHADA

Pledge of Allegiance

I pledge to defend my home and family from all enemies both foreign and domestic.

Here I sit perched with a bird's eye view holding my rifle, one scope and the dreams of a people so boldly molested.

Pouting with damnation on our lips,

we sip poisonous reparations as blood tinged termites soil our crypts.

Suffering on the edge of extinction,

we draw our line in the sand with an eminent domain distinction.

Not one foot back and nothing less than what is rightfully ours forward.

We sowed the seeds of their fields, now it's time to burn down their orchard.

They slept while our feet pounded pavement meant for enslavement,

then fed us lies from their tables and kept us like orphans locked in the basement.

Screaming only to give proof of existence,

their constant assistance upon distance shattered our unity and lowered our resistance.

They spent years creating the illusion of a self-made protagonist,

mean-while our chemical make-up is repurposed with our very essence as the catalyst.

Far from a fiction or the dark ramblings of an anarchist,

they send terms and speak of equality but I don't negotiate with terrorists.

As dawn looms on the horizon I see my adversary lying in wait,

concealed with murderous intentions, no mistakes this time, he plans to clean the slate.

I close my eyes one last time but it's not forgiveness I seek, only that my aim be true,

that for every shell ejected, let their numbers dwindle by two.

As I open my eyes I place my weapon against my shoulder and let these tired bones support its weight,

surrender was never an option and deliverance came just a little too late.

I pledge to defend my home and family from all enemies both foreign and domestic...

I lived for what we were and died for what will become, so that when their end comes they'd never forget it...

15

Until...

Until the last word is spoken....

Until the final bone is broken....

Until the last tear rolls down from my cheek,...

Until this rope relieves me of my ability to speak,...

Until the truth is exposed as a lie....

Until age removes the hate from my eye....

Until the silence flows through my veins and cascades into the street....

Until I can't be the man you despise and the one that cries alone in his sleep....

Until the rain stops and the clouds give way....

Until the pain from these esoteric secrets are too much to bear and I can't stay....

Until I no longer see the end because I've finally lost the race....

Until the faults of the son, the father can no longer replace....

Until my spirit eases on into oblivion....

Until the hope of all men dies in the absence of an Olympian....

Until I can see past the hurt and sadness that scars my sight....

Until suicide becomes a viable answer and the chemical reactions begin to ignite....

Until looking off this terrace isn't enough and my body begins to descend....

Until the air moves past my skin and I feel normal again....

Until my existence is erased and carried away by the wind....

Until I can finally let go and be released of yesterday's sin....

Until....

Requiem

Out of breath,

bent over in duress, looking back... one down, two more on the left.

Blind fire in the dark, about as accurate as a pull out,

quite as kept but payback will bring the wolf out.

Punishment sought for dispersal of verbal pestilence,

recompense taught as a mandatory inheritance.

Young'un stepped up his weight but couldn't carry it,

the struggle is hard but this loss broke the proletariat.

So engulfed in his grief, robbed of his light, he answered back for this unspeakable theft,

wounded, blurry muzzle flash in the distance, he screams out... two down... one more on the left.

Let Them Come

The dawn sky, citrus in its exterior,
ominously reflecting the malice coursing through my interior.

Scanning the horizon, I see not peace but war in the distance,
 against the domination of subjugation, I shall give every resistance

The people are ready and our gates substantial,
our enemies are many but their future lies upon my mantle.

They've propagated deceit for generations,
now their offspring await their end in a field of fabrications.

A blustery wind blows through these cobblestone streets so cold you question its neutrality,
alone but together in this great old city, not even mother nature can test our mortality.

I rest perched like a gargoyle alongside this tower gazing down at the souls below,
I see terror attempting to take hold but having no fertile ground to grow.

The men firm in their resolve, plan and strategize clutching large weapons,
while the women secure the young, stand adjacent but are the second line of vengeance.

For no one's hands will be clean, the halls of the church will have no attendance,
forgiveness is not required and there is no need for repentance.

No wrong will be committed this day or screams of righteous indignation from a soon to be martyr,
they came to our land, violated our border, they can lay down their arms but will receive no quarter.

Just then, the first stone cast!

A near miss but it would not be the last.

I have no intention of waiting until their aim become accurate,

the order is given "let their blood and the soil in equal parts begin to commensurate!".

The ground shook as we marched out toward what seemed like our destiny,

walking amongst them, sensing their heart and minds, you can't help but notice the perfect symmetry.

It's one thing to perceive your adversary but to face them in the flesh is another,

without hesitation we engaged with the goal to maim, destroy and at the very least make them suffer.

Swords clanged against shield and bone,

cries of agony, were silenced by an ax making itself home.

Once separated by color of origin, now sheer will is the only identifier,

we fought to exhaustion, strength gone but not one knee dropped, we would not tire.

In the end, bodies scattered about, faces unrecognizable,

we won the day but the loss of life was sizeable.

We wished none of this and mourn the deaths of all,

they challenged our very existence, we would not fall.

We returned them to the Earth from whence they came, for this battle is done,

we will not run to a fight but defeat isn't an option, so if there is another, let them come...

The Revolution Must Be Televised

I died on January 20th, 1973 from a projectile of hate,

on April 4th, 1968 I was slain in the name of ignorance in an attempt to wipe the slate.

I succumbed to my wounds on September 26th, 1959 due to granting another respect.

on June 12th, 1963 a bullet pierced my back because of change the opposition couldn't accept.

November 22nd, 1963 a conspiracy took aim on me before I could finish creating something better.

On April 15th, 1865, I was taken from this earth, my only crime...trying to bring a country together.

I was shot by an officer on Christmas Day 2015, an accident but a tragedy nonetheless.

I never left Fruitvale Station on New Year's Day 2009 because tolerance hasn't meant progress.

On July 15th of 2013 I was tortured and killed for supporting the right to choose.

I was left for dead and passed away on October 12th, 1998 when fear caused another innocent to lose.

I fell alongside heroes on September 11th, 2001 when cowards endeavored to bring down a nation,

I didn't make it home on June 12th, 2016 due to one man's delusional, despicable personal degradation.

I am you and we are them,

these aren't just lines in a poem, they're a portrait of beauty this world chose to expend.

No matter your color, race or religion, our very existence unites us,

whether you believe in forever or a silent void, the taking of a life should ignite us.

We fight for ideologies that lack true etiology since the psychology is warped by historical cosmetology,

the only true constant is our biology that links us no matter your terminology.

I write this not to sway you to act, for that's your decision to make,

but to ask yourself, "how much more can you take?"

The last straw was too long ago and relief won't come soon enough.

There's no politician behind the podium, just a human tired of having to adjust.

I'm not above violence but anger just breeds retaliation,

I'm willing to turn the other cheek but if it's an eye for an eye, then we stumble blindly into annihilation.

Keep the side arm on your hip but holster it until needed,

with your hands now free, triage the wounded and the socioeconomic defeated.

We're not the Red Cross but we can be an army that brings salvation,

the first step is realizing our differences are our greatest innovation.

Our beliefs don't have to be a prison but a garden to develop and cultivate,

we're one in the same, so let our variations pollinate.

But if all fails and the lights dim, let them know we'll be coming in force,

we've been married in dysfunction for decades, it's time for a divorce.

Guerrilla tactics are a strategy but we'll be knocking at your front door,

every faith, race and denomination united with millions on standby if we need more.

It won't be a temporary emotion or in response to a singular violation,

it'll be the physical iteration of frustration from years of concealed desecration.

The cameras will be rolling, not for publicity but for all to bear witness,

it'll be an open and honest record, no algorithm needed to decrypt this.

No date selected, some targets in mind,

this day will come though and all intolerance, ignorance and hatred will be out of time.

There is an Olive Branch that I fear is just too far out of your reach,

the Revolution must be televised or this is mere rhetoric and we become mute...without speech.

Chapter 2

BREATHE

呼吸

RESPIRER

نفس

ДЫШАТЬ

RESPIRAR

Here I Am

Here I am,

standing at those same crossroads.

Here I am,

wishing for a different outcome while the same grief just reloads.

Here I am,

clutching my fists in anger over the same mistakes.

Here I am,

regretting past actions and promising change no matter what it takes.

Here I am,

lost in despair but knowing the way all too well.

Here I am,

positioned over my own corpse and being disgusted by the smell.

Here I am,

surrounded by senseless depression and pitfalls of my own construction.

Here I am,

kneeling in this somber place with this razorblade to my throat praying for no interruption.

Here I am,

again and again and again,

Here I am,

asking you to let me go so I don't have to pretend.

Here I am,

requesting that you think less of me and acknowledge the same disappointment that I have.

Here I am,

pleading that you accept this apology for the courage I just couldn't grasp.

Here I am,

demanding that you close your arms and let me walk alone!

Here I am,

begging that you understand that this time I won't be coming home.

Here I am,

writing these same vacillating words as before.

Here I am,

leaving behind the pen and the pad, saying goodbye and finally, closing the door.

Blissful Ignorance

Sufficient suspicion clouded the opposition,

similar to the religious conviction that created the crucifixion.

Societal norms collapsing in collegiate fashion,

erudition wide spread, still many offer no ration.

Strained consumption increasing normal conscription,

subsequent assessment inspiring post dereliction.

Financial exchange daring to bear witness,

currency constrictions toxic, causing sickness.

Lungs stained with intangible opulence,

many more tombstones engraved as a consequence.

Cubicle confinement distressing the unconventional,

an even playing field cautioning the intellectual.

Emotions given, received and dismissed in the blink of an eye,

last one standing is often the next to die.

Exaggeration implied but absent from this monologue,

blind without presence of malice is the purpose of our dialogue.

Frozen beyond the thought of all potential,

the light glowing just past the wind regurgitates the consequential.

The stipulation of remaining silent to gain ground is gone,

conceding position for the sake of another won't validate which side you're on.

As we take each breath, never stop to contemplate the last,

appreciate each second because a moment, is all we have.

Sometimes

Sometimes I think you're the source of my pain.

Sometimes I think you're the one to blame.

Sometimes I wish you were mine.

Sometimes I think I'm running out of time.

Sometimes I hope someday you'll understand.

Sometimes I just want to hold your hand.

Sometimes I can't wait to feel the softness of your hair.

Sometimes I wish I could caress your skin with tender loving care.

Sometimes I wish my feelings would change.

Sometimes I think our relationship is totally strange.

Sometimes I look and I see you as my future.

Sometimes I look and see you as my abuser.

Sometimes I wish you would tell me what's true.

Sometimes I wish I could complete you.

Sometimes all we have are the dreams that fill our day.

Sometimes when we reach for the stars, gravity tends to get in the way.

Sometimes what we want most, will hurt us the deepest.

Sometimes I wish I could turn back time but I would only repeat this.

Sometimes you must wish, gain and lose.

Sometimes no matter how hard you try, your heart breaks the rules.

Sometimes I think you're the source of my pain and the one to blame.

Sometimes at night I look up and pray you feel the same.

Words To Live By...

A man is a man, not because of circumstance but because of what he becomes in spite of it.

A man seeks help when he needs it and provides it whenever possible.

A man is not just a rock of strength but a foundation for growth.

A man doesn't apologize for being wrong but for not being able to see the right.

A man knows not fear but caution.

A man doesn't cry tears of sorrow but does shed the pain, so light can take its place.

A man is stoic in all things but unafraid to love another.

A man is power and courage but gives respect and support.

A man will take a moment to realize a mistake rather than misstep for an eternity.

A man is wise but accepts true enlightenment when given.

A man is drive and ambition but also kindness and compassion.

A man is both an example and a way of life, only time will judge his legacy.

A man is firm in his conviction but gives room for clarity.

A man is sanctuary from the storm and shelter for those in need.

A man is who, how and what he makes of himself.

A man is strength, love, wisdom and purpose but above all else...

A man is there.

Chapter 3

Incarcerated Introspection

被囚禁的反省

Introspection incarcérée

سجن المسكن

Интроспекция заключенных

Introspection incarcérée

When The Low Points Come

When you're just below expectation…

When it's that last memory before separation…

When you realize your failure…

When those empty platitudes lose favor…

When the promises of something better are gone…

When the future you thought so right, becomes so wrong.

When you can stand back up on your own but still need to pretend…

When you cripple yourself just to feel again…

When you open old soars just to let them bleed…

When you won't let the new cuts heal, hoping death to proceed…

When the addiction became the prescription…

When the affliction stopped being the contradiction…

When you can't let go because you won't concede it's over…

When you're at the bar spinning eternity in circles wishing you were sober…

When ten seconds changed your whole perspective…

When you're too close to those pills and feeling reflective…

When once blissful thoughts scar you numb…

When you must create mountains just to overcome…

When the flashbacks only contain harmful images, you can't forget…

When your first breath in the morning is one of regret…

When old pictures only bring back the pain…

When the shame erases the integrity from your name…

When you removed the lies and were disgusted by what remained…

When you've been beaten and life has taken all you've gained…

When you squeezed first but desired to be second...

When you're praying for forgiveness still clutching your weapon...

When writing about the hurt no longer relieves the compulsion...

When the self-hate clouds your judgment and only the quiet will satisfy the revulsion...

...

When you can finally accept that it might just be your fault...

When you understand that a mistake doesn't define you...the suffering can begin to halt...

When you recognize that you're not okay but you will be...

When you figure out it's alright to move on and stop feeling guilty...

When you've travelled away from the sadness and doubt until you can no longer tell how far...

When you accept that no one and nothing can take from the person you are...

When those closest have turned their backs and still you move forward, alone...

When you've out grown adolescent fantasies and found your way home...

When you realize the foundation you've been searching for, is the strength you already had...

When you can find joy in another but it's belief in yourself that makes you glad.

When you can accept this life, although not what you planned, is still beautiful because it's yours...

When you can give back to those you've taken from realizing there still may be some closed doors...

When you can find happiness, in the thought of tomorrow...

When the grieving is over and you can shed the sorrow...

When you can nullify the inner conflict and replace it with ambition...

When the choice to walk and smile again is your decision...

When you're ready to let go and perceive the memories without reaction...

When you're done reliving the same story to justify inaction...

When you can give light to the darkness and finally become free...

When you uncover the path away from this place...please come back for me...

I Can't Be The Only One

I was by the lake, visualizing a perfect world riding the ripples in the water.

There's not much time left to daydream as the days have gotten shorter.

Out there, in the solitude of a breeze I could be him...

That is, I can be me...I can...be...

As you skim through these words, would you do me a kindness?

Please do not judge this point of view, for it suffers from blindness.

Frozen in a dimly lit space as beautiful as the snow,

shouting with no voice, only self-mutilation can I show.

*And yet...*I can't be the only one that still hopes for that warm embrace,

for that instant that will wipe away the tears tattooed upon my face.

Like a corsage for a prom I'll never attend, my feelings stay exposed to the air,

*And yet...*I can't be the only one at the water's edge...alone, cradling the warmth of despair.

I thought that if I gave all of me, every ounce of myself it would be enough!

How can you gamble on a guarantee so tangible just to find out it was all a bluff?

After you've given so much, there's nothing left but the shell of what used to be...

After you've opened your heart, your mind, your soul...to what, could never be...

*And yet...*I can't be the only one, sinking motionless in quicksand,

caressing a scar from previous loss, longing...scared to extend my hand.

I recognize the process for progress requires better prospects,

but the outlook is minimal when we only see each other as objects.

If I'm merely a means to an end, how do we resolve the equation?

I've lost all purpose; my heart has given in to cessation...

*And yet...*I can't be the only one waiting in the shadows for the anguish to subside,

be with me, one last time, push me below the waves...let me slip away with the tide.

Stone

Dawns of deep dreams deepen debts made by a lost heart.

Sharp shrieks from mental sharks shred anatomy of every part.

Looking like a lump of clay through the dark,

claiming calm collective thoughts, when it's your own actions that leave a mark.

Daily doses of damnation form the flesh not spoken of,

handling harmful material six feet under while protected from above.

Manipulating my mind by moving mountains that were once in my way,

only invisible instruments invade promiscuity intended for another day.

Fireworks flying, felt from firmly placed nerves,

courage giving correction continuously keeping my roads straight from curves.

Even though young, yearning for days gone, for another chance,

weakened, wasting away, I wished for another dance.

Vulnerable to the violation I unwittingly volunteered for,

visible to a viper that releases its venom to a virgin of falling to the floor.

Virtual variable vinegar giving me a new taste but breaking my vertebrae,

a vampire bleeding me through valves, giving vibrations that rippled through the bay.

Minute mirrors reflect mirages that mimic urges of long ago.

A memorial measures memories of accomplishments.

Maternal materialistic ideals materialize many times during the night.

Malevolent malice masks truth making my path clear yet so blinded.

Rivers ripping new rugged terrain through old ground...

Previous plagues coming back placing pressures unseen...

Sunlight breaking through the fog that once covered my surface...

Seeing my breath in the cold I realize I can no longer remain as this...Stone.

Nourishment

These walls seem deeper than the last.

The blood has a different smell than before.

The silence in this room is breaking me!

It's so dark...

So vacant...

My bare feet rest on a wet floor but I have no answer.

Last night's rat, last night's dinner.

But wait, I haven't satisfied you yet!

To believe I could ever be so rude, do not take as a threat.

I seem so important now but where were you when the tears wouldn't end?

When you put your hand on my shoulder and called yourself my friend.

Is it coming back or must I refresh your recollection?

You said I'd be better under your direction.

The hair on my arms have been shaved clean,

now the designation you gave me can be seen.

Scars like rainbows cover my exterior.

The thought of others seeing them makes me feel inferior.

My tongue soaked from licking my wounds,

dry are my eyes like a desert, lost in the dunes.

Feeling this hand approach my throat,

I awake to my own aggression as my body attempts to cope.

No surprise is my desire to be free.

No small challenge is this barrier blocking me.

If I take two steps back, the water will consume my body.

If take two steps forward, the ground will accept my corpse.

I only beg that you now give me your honesty.

I only ask now, that you give me my nourishment.

Credo ut intelligam

Open to every idea, diligent in my observance,

on my knees nightly, my mind and your will, in constant convergence.

Invisible walls surrounding my perception,

you tell me the outside is a wasteland, that you'll provide protection.

I can walk among them but forever remain intangible,

to exist but never grow in their light and deem your every action infallible.

My psyche robbed of development in any other direction,

my soul, merely a vessel awaiting your omnipotent selection.

My purpose, still unbeknownst to me,

I toil in internal conflict, pondering if I really know what it is to be free?

You warn that beyond these borders lie only shame and annihilation,

without you, there is only confusion and desolation.

You reign through trepidation and guarded solidarity,

you lead by postulation and despise questions on granularity.

Obedience not by loyalty but through consequence,

if this is the path to salvation then I have succumbed to the failings of my own incompetence.

It all seems so clear, in the absence that is your presence,

but separated and alone, the isolation breeds insecurity and the need for acceptance.

Subjugation or liberation through devastation?

To be loved and limited or exiled for selfish affirmation?

To be owner of my universe or just another star in the sky?

to these choices I look to my heart for an answer but with no reply.

I believe, so that I may understand,

I don't seek to become a god, only to exist as a man.

<u>Consequences</u>

We always believe they'll be a tomorrow to make up for today.

Another sunrise to apologize for what you never intended to say.

We forget that even though the hourglass is slow moving it's cracked,

inside forgiveness, resides last night's attack.

Even with the best of intention we can miss the clarity component,

life is merciful but we can burn on the sidelines waiting for enrollment.

Stand but be willing to crawl for the right reason,

strength is honorable but betrayal of your heart can render your existence to its completion.

It's Okay...

I see where you are because I've been there before,

it seems like every day I try but I just can't open that door.

Locked in this void of despair and loss,

I can't imagine a way out that wouldn't require a high cost.

I know about the long days of sadness and depression,

the constant replays of painful moments that bring about the aggression.

I know about the "what if's" and the guilt driven envisioned humiliations,

I've felt that same self-hatred and pity inspired isolation that bring about the ideations.

I've occupied your same position but I'm not you,

I won't presume to know your anguish or sponsor you to continue.

I'm not your counselor, your therapist or even a friend,

I'm an ear in the silence for you to scream to when it's close to the end.

I'm not a parent, a teacher or a role model promising a new day,

I just want you to know, if it ever gets to be too much and there's no other way... it's okay...

If the memories only bring agony and tomorrow's only possibility is tragedy... I understand.

If the room is burning and the ledge is the only exit....I will be there wherever you land.

No one knows your struggle and no one can fight your demons if the opponent is your soul.

Hope is an invention of the spectator; a bystander can only speculate on the horrors you behold.

This isn't a white flag, nor open arms to your end,

this is an echo of sorrow time couldn't mend.

But please... before you let it all go and you swallow that pill or take that leap,

balance the scales a little and let them comprehend the secrets you keep.

Don't go into that abyss without making an impact,

take just one last chance to turn their perfect world into an abstract.

No matter what you've been through or the torture you've endured you meant something!

Your time here counted because through it all, you held on while your world was crumbling.

If this is the end of your journey, don't go quietly,

if hell awaits you, go defiantly!

Before you raise that weapon upright just hear me out,

I know it's been lonely but don't give into the doubt.

You've tried it on your own and failure is all you can see,

but tunnel vision is blinding because there's one more option if you'll come with me.

The fact that you're here isn't weakness or a lack of courage to defend,

it's the beginning, if my perception you'll allow me to lend.

Yesterday's sin is not why you're in this place but merely fuel to the flames already lit,

there's an underlying battle that resides within you where the scars manifest and begin to strip.

I can't relieve the symptoms but I can tell you the result,

no matter what happens in this life they're arrogance won't bring it to a halt!

We'll take our scrapes and losses and carry on in spite,

fuck giving up, we're going to war if this is our last night!

Those voices in your head that were once against you will now sound the alarm,

discharged from our mind are those thoughts that plagued your existence and only brought harm.

Our past is our past and there's nothing we can do to change it,

we can only move forward in force making our presence known, they'll take it how they take it!

Apologies are for mistakes, these are corrections to our wrongs,

we'll shower the walls with our message, their bones can write the songs.

This isn't a call to arms, it's a demand for action.

Don't leave this world until you've gotten your satisfaction.

It's not us versus them,

it's your world they're living in.

So let your declaration say "I'm here!" and let no other words be spoken.

Then take the last piece of you, hold it close and leave the remnants of yesterday lost and broken.

As I sit here beside you, know that you're not alone and my hand is here to stay,

but if this room with no walls begins to close in too close, I want you to know... it's okay...

Chapter 4

I DO

我做

أنا إفعل

JE FAIS

Я ДЕЛАЮ

IN LOVING MEMORY

HAGO

One Last Conversation

I love you, you know that?	*I can't do this again…*
I trusted you…	*Please don't pretend…*
I was there for you!	*And I appreciated your presence.*
I gave you my all!	*And now you want vengeance?*
You make it seem so easy…	*It's not, but I can let go.*
Isn't it tearing you apart?	*Wishing it did, won't make it so.*
I wanted forever…	*But all we'd have is regret.*
I bought you a ring…	*You never said…I…I can't accept*
Did you ever care?	*Of course…but now it's done.*
You were my world!	*You need light but I can't be your sun.*
So is this the end of our chapter?	*For us, there is no "Happily Ever After".*
I love you, you know?	*I know, but it just doesn't matter…*

Cornea

Soft as elegance from beautiful lips,

gracious in its pronunciation,

oh what a sensation to be the rim of that glass, as she sips.

Bound by a promise, he can only admire from afar,

without options,

he observes as a silhouette miles away, distant as a star.

Voluntary seclusion enlightening those in observance,

motionless in response,

most don't recognize the disturbance.

He remained in silence and gave no allowance for scandal,

the crowds waited,

 he stole glances of her beauty but only what he could handle.

Such a charmed life exhibited but nothing more than a mirage,

poignant seclusion,

shattered aspirations form an unhealthy collage.

Although withering from within he projects strength to those in attendance,

damaged beyond repair,

he stands alone, ever present, an echo of remembrance.

With You

Rare flower in the garden blooming without praise,

like a five-step waltz in "A" minor, observed from an obstructed gaze.

Partially grown though hesitant to experiment,

soft and delicate, sweet is its scent, like peppermint.

May almost over, February on its way,

eight months in between or maybe just a long day.

 Her petal now fully formed; propagated pollination propels the population,

isolated by the separation she gives into her grief over an absent constellation.

Bent in distress, an indignity unseen,

mapped in evolution, a princess to never be queen.

Solitary but solidified in solidarity,

she was now one with the garden, their union erasing all depravity.

Her pain...

I saw her there...

Standing in defiance of the inevitable.

There she would remain,

clinging to the hollowness and his acts so detestable.

In this shadowy place, in this vacuum, she waits for him,

in this public forum she lays bare her agony!

Her scars, visible through her tattered clothing,

revealing narrative across her battered body like hieroglyphic molding.

As the wind blows across the bruises she cries out for him!

Reticence being the only reply,

she resides in this space for only he can release her spirit.

Her allegiance is eternal, he need only say the word and she will give it...

As the birds circle, her skin tears open from ulcerating complicity,

she glances back and for just a second, she smiles with sincerity.

Her obligation met, she surrendered to serenity,

for the only misery is ours and the only sedition be our own insecurity.

Though her tears keep her captive and heart breaks like ocean waves against the rocks,

her soul is with him and although lost, she is forever found in her pain.

He will never be in that moment, at that time or share that space,

but she will sing for him and he will listen...

I saw her there...

Where I've stood for so long,

if you close your eyes and accept the loss, you can be one with her pain, until all of it is gone...

Chapter 5
BRAZEN WOLVES

LOBOS BRONCEOSENTONCES

SAND PAPER

Looks like we've got another one,
looks young...fresh meat.
He doesn't realize he's being watched,
he'll be approached near the kitchen, they won't be discreet.

It'll be a smile, a nudge and then a suggestion,
non-negotiable, inevitable silent aggression.
They'll test him but it's not a gamble,
they pick their targets well, this life can be more that most can handle.

A hoe check ain't always necessary, brings too much attention,
a lame duck will turn into a June bug for protection.
Crazy part is, most guys here aren't punks, just prison wolves doing what they gotta,
the others stay on that brake fluid making they Cadillac feel better than the Ramada.

These fish get dropped off with nothing more than a survival kit and a permanent pocket,
only here for a bullet...end up doing the Dutch cuz somebody's filling it and C.O.'s don't stop it.
Saw several opt for P.C. but you never know if you're sitting next to a torpedo,
dem spider monkeys go three-knee-deep for a few bats and some pruno.

They bus'em in younger and younger, most not built for this,
I've been here longer than I can remember, a life jolt...still got the marks on my wrist.
The vampires said I caught the monster doing my first dime,
back then it was harder, you felt everyday of your time.

Now all I see is one day, it'll be a back-door parole but beyond the gates,
I've recorded it all, so they can line the walls with my story in the casket that awaits.
This life will take you, one way or the other,
It's almost time...I think I'm done now...this last page, should be just enough to cover.

To The Last...

Narrowed spiteful insurrection just below temptation set aside for your damnation,

stood tall by your side while mutinous intentions permeated your entire nation.

Guarded your six when you couldn't count the cost,

with you down to the last, so you never felt the loss.

I held my position when the written disposition of opposition fell upon your description,

then rewrote their composition from what was hidden before invisible armaments made a proposition.

Touched less ground than us but spoke with eloquence of endurance and decision,

while your purview was of a bird's view as we expired through your prism.

For you nothing more than a memory forgotten for a century,

but old wounds still bleed when treachery is an accessory.

Duplicity

Judgment resides on my hip,

hollowed passengers destroy with collateral damage as they expand from the tip.

Heavy footed soldiers approach my position with preemptive predicated precision,

eternally the unseen contortionist, my movements decrease sight from their elongated predictions.

Street lanterns like night torches against the pitch-black sky back drop,

these provide only an illustration for the outline of tomorrow's topic as the coroners talk shop.

Gazing from the shadows like an observing conspirator,

I spy their route of ascent, waiting with this bird holding its seven cargo and chambered ambassador.

Sampling that which gives me breath I inhale the pretense and exhale the betrayal,

caught behind enemy lines I will not fall, I will not fail, send an army, this exterior is not frail!

Their plot exposed, they deem retribution for the collusion,

but my eyes were brought upon their deceit only in the midst of the confusion.

One deal too many, a second misplaced,

now the memory of my vision they try to erase.

She never saw it coming….she was an innocent,

they took my world away and deemed it irrelevant.

As they advance in formation on my former,

flanking their location, I exposed weakness, causing disorder.

In retort they decimate with the intention to annihilate,

flooding my station with slugs built to exterminate.

I crawled behind a parked car, glass shattered from above, bullets let off like loss sentiments,

I blind-fired hitting one, which enraged them more….like they really needed the encouragement.

Another clip down, one to go,

I reload hoping the lights in the windows above are enjoying the show.

Then in the distance, the sound from a siren,

its wail, almost as sweet as the sun rising over the horizon.

Not to be deterred, my aggressors move in knowing time is a factor,

I get up realizing I've been hit in the leg, adrenaline will have to do...I'll deal with the pain after.

Leaving cover, I limped into an alley alongside a building,

a shot narrowly missing my head cemented intentions that they were more than willing.

Half-way down this dead end, a reflection from a red and blue light,

the screams of "Police! Stop!" from the street, provided relief and an end to this terrible night.

Suddenly, the unmistakable cocking from the hammer of a gun,

dropping my own, slowly I turned, only to see my entire world undone.

I fell back against a cold surface, my eyes fixed up at a starless sky,

he yelled "snitch!" as he came closer to give his aim another try.

He stood to the right, raised the barrel in line with my face,

as he began to squeeze, I produced a back-up weapon from its hidden space.

Right arm broken, my left was ready for reply,

unseen and swift, he stumbled back before knowing why.

Two rounds put the assailant down,

fearing it may not be over, I staggered upward from the ground.

I knelt down next to his body, removed a shield from my pocket and placed it on his chest,

with blood pouring from his mouth and gasping for air, I informed him..."you're under arrest".

Long Road To Nowhere

He ran out the back door like tomorrow didn't exist,

regretting the last twenty-four hours but we all knew the risk.

The streets empty but crowded with echoes and ricochets,

caught up in last night's betrayal, he prays for wisdom and better days.

Marked by inspiration, targeted for decapitation,

Elias resolved for disappearance, rather than cardiac cessation.

Once promised a place amongst the greatest, now slated for early retirement,

he was a product and victim of his own hostile environment.

Smiled and gave credence to the belief we could overcome,

but talked with gaps in his mouth leaving crumbs until he was done.

Not just another soldier but "Semper fi" until his last breath,

forever faithful, he drank damnation until nothing was left.

Long days of pillaging properties in search of autonomy,

bullet broken bones lay at his feet just to enhance his economy.

All the while plotting on escape,

too afraid to take it, maybe just too afraid to wake.

Knowing his opponents are approaching from the rear,

he descends into a "vacant" where murmurs from ghosts still bend his ear.

Weak rotted wooden steps slowed the progress of his pursuers,

at the top, nowhere to go, he peers over the ledge realizing he's exhausted all maneuvers.

Finally, facing his fate he accepts his end but doesn't romanticize the beginning,

with his hands in the air, he gives them his back and......

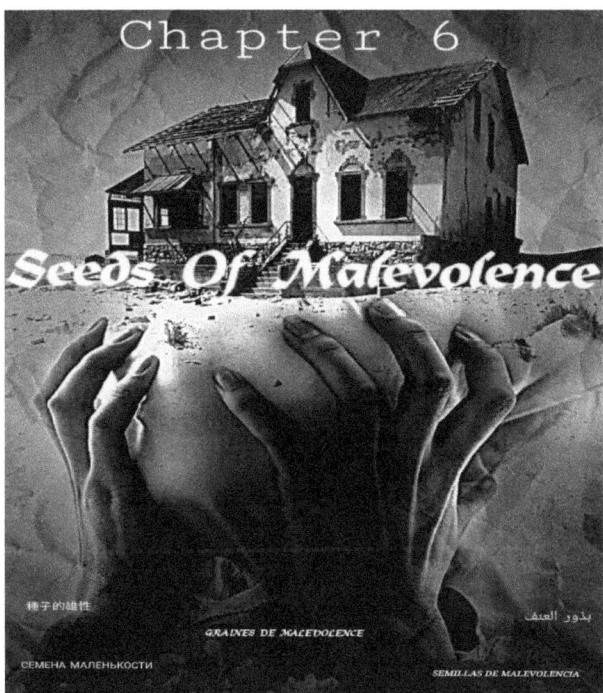

Chapter 6

Seeds Of Malevolence

稗子的雄性

بذور العنف

GRAINES DE MALEVOLENCE

СЕМЕНА МАЛЕНЬКОСТИ

SEMILLAS DE MALEVOLENCIA

Run II

Lying supine deep in thought, my eyelids embrace my face as my mind rambles about in mis-direction,

the rain beating against my window provides serenity but gives silence to the cruelest of intention.

As I repose on these cushions made of leather in this dark tiny space I call home,

for just a moment I awake, to a glimpse of a shadow not my own.

As it moved along the wall, the lightning announced its presence,

frozen in fear, I weighed reality against premature anxiety from adolescence.

In an instant it disappeared, almost as quickly as it came,

lost was my worry, replaced only by shame at being frightened by thoughts only a child would entertain.

I expelled a quiet sigh of relief and once again fell into a state of tranquility,

not realizing that within a few feet lurked an evil that towards me, held so much hostility.

Suddenly the crack of thunder startled me alert to the visualization of a man standing over me,

caught in the moment, our eyes met and I knew the same again, is what I'd never be.

From his position behind my place of rest he thrusts his right hand downward on to my neck,

crushing my throat with all his strength without an ounce of regret.

I responded in defiance grabbing him, attempting to pull his hand away,

with his left hand he reached down and pulled out a small knife to quiet my resolve and execute his prey.

Seeing my struggle about to become futile,

I forced my body to the floor turning this immobile victim a lot more agile.

As I quickly stumble to my feet and get my bearings,

my assailant closes the distance, all the while never loosing eye contact, just viciously staring.

I pleaded with him to take all that I have except my life, hoping for a pardon,

he merely tightened the grip on his weapon and his gaze just seemed to sharpen.

But suddenly his eyes turned from anger to contemplation,

it was as if my pleas for mercy had broken through and gave reason for hesitation.

His head angled down and for the first time interrupted his intense focus of me from his sight,

he appeared almost limp, with his arms at his side and his weapon calm, far from taking flight.

Stock-still, afraid to antagonize this intruder in my home,

I examine my options, glancing a path toward the door, unsure if my plan of escape is known.

Understanding the phrase "now or never" to be my guide, I took off like a bullet on a mission,

only to find my guest thought the same and anticipated my decision.

I felt a great force pull me back and hurl me to the floor,

with my plan now turned fatal mistake, I saw no way out and his brutal assault began once more.

We struggled for dominance in a fight I was all too unprepared for,

between hope and terror, we thrashed about with only frenzied punches and bruises to keep score.

Feeling like an eternity but lasting only seconds,

faced with extermination I fought to the last, using my fists as weapons.

I finally gained ground through slurries of physical exchanges,

at one point afraid, now on the offensive as the blood within rages.

Numb to the pain I grabbed a shard of broken glass from the floor,

fueled by anger I jabbed it into my enemy's throat until his blood began to pour.

Again and again it ripped through his skin, tearing open his neck like an aluminum can,

finally I stopped, dropped my tool of death, got up from his beaten body and ran.

In my ears I could still hear him gurgling for a breath,

I exited through his entrance, each step fumbled as if my perception couldn't grasp the depth.

Off balance, almost delirious,

feeling fragmented, my thoughts dark and insidious.

Dazed and unsteady I made my way down the fire escape,

too terrified to look back from fear his form from behind me, would take shape.

At last I reached the street, shattered, bloody; my freedom almost too real to accept,

limping as fast I could, I saw a light, I was nearing the final stretch.

As I moved forward, crowds and bright lights began to come into focus,

like a bright summer day in a large field, full of locusts.

Just then, a loud voice commanded me to stop,

it demanded my cooperation and told me to drop.

Submitting to this authority I knelt to my knees,

suddenly silence and all I noticed was yellow tape blowing in the breeze.

A short distance away I observed my position surrounded by lawmen and civilians,

I knew my plight that night was perilous but didn't expect help by the millions.

Then the voice yells for me to drop the weapon and put my face to the ground,

I look at my hand and in it, is where the weapon of my enemy is found.

Confused and perplexed, I begin to shake and panic as the blood drips from the knife,

could it be….could it be I was the intruder attempting to take a life?

Tears began to fall as I began to break,

I accepted the nightmare was of my own making but I was very much awake.

I robbed someone of the greatest gift while trapped in my own mind,

I recollected my last steps, plotting destruction and the empty bottle I left behind.

My heart seized and I collapsed under the weight of my culpability,

reality filled my lungs and I drowned in a sea of instability.

Only to awaken in this room in which I can barely breathe,

no windows, locked doors, restrained but just enough room to grieve.

Though despondent, I noticed the silhouette of a guard standing outside the door.

I'll get him close; loosen a strap, grab his weapon, then leave his body on the floor.

Such a noise though, someone may come to inquire,

more bodies would be nice but the time for my escape is beginning to expire.

Robed in the clothes of my jailer, I proceeded in plain sight,

some simple nods and gestures and I'm back out into the night.

If they were less concerned with my condition rather than my potential,

they would've imprisoned me instead of caring for me in a neighborhood so residential.

I was like them once but then he came,

innocent turned butcher, our goals became the same.

I can feel the urge coming, it pervades through my veins,

the hunt begins once more, my soul gone, let there be no mercy for what remains.

Night Terrors

I pray that you bear my appearance through this transformation in age,

though I have no ill will in my heart, I can't contain the rage.

Begging your pardon but do you have any change perhaps?

I'm long from attendance at a table and I tire of scraps.

With your permission, I'll sleep at the base of your feet and have only what you give as shelter,

I mean so little to so few, let me assume the role of your helper.

I cannot clean, I am unable to build but I am of great company,

a slave to the domestic but practice total autonomy.

Still... the pain is great and so is the hour,

the illumination of innocence has set upon the tower.

I covet its magnificent beauty as the blade slides across your wrist,

quiet please! screams will only make me insist.

Let it be slow but quick,

angle your head to the south, for the shock may make you sick.

I was your friend, your confidant and now executioner,

you've rested your trust in Themis' daughter but have found no refuge in her.

This is the consequence of falsely imposed confidence,

you alluded to my depravity and savagery believing it was due to incompetence.

Such a final verdict could only be derived from surface examination,

without hesitation you displayed machinations of an adolescent created imagination.

You deserve not life, not foul,

so I will end you in my assumed barbarity and look to the moon and howl.

Rest in peace or lie in agony,

I'll remember to tip my hat as I leave your grave, your majesty....

34

You don't know my pain...

Let rhyme and reason go and you'll see we're not the same...

She was my every thought and concern...

Thought it was love but it wasn't my turn...

Unnatural sentiment unloaded to my detriment...

Speech without sound as my heart forms an impediment...

Evening's traversing familiar ground in hopes of a connection...

Insidious inclinations churning in my peripheral, praying for a correction...

Forever and a day or at least that was the vernacular used...

Then to be thrown and bludgeoned with more than my pride bruised...

Ascension in the late with a silent presentation may solve the equation...

I pronounce myself lost and hold back but slowly losing my hesitation...

No accusation to extend for the fault is my own...

No new realization, the outcome is well known...

Tomorrow came but with yesterday's intention...

I turned hope into a lie and burned its ashes hoping for redemption...

I walked a broken path because it was a familiar descent...

I probably would've followed her into oblivion but never knowing what it meant...

Southern Exposure

Give me the strength to accept this humiliation,

as I wait by these rusty old tracks, six years post sanitation.

The sky gray with mixed emotions,

my mind racing, the only path generated is littered with Trojans.

I exaggerate the condition of the invisible individual in hopes that his plight might stick with you,

for only the lonely live life in the light clutching the same ritual.

So quickly I threw this bloody dagger across an Acheronian like alley,

chills as warm as a sun break, travel up my epidermis simulating a sensation of "happy".

I stare at your reluctance and can only contemplate an insidious action,

I gave you me and therefore everything but you accepted only the hollow frame expecting traction.

Crawling only for spectacle, I find my behavior unacceptable,

the way out rests its head in the nearest trash receptacle.

More often than not the plot sickens,

tortured into shock, the feeble mind glistens.

Captivated by a caption of capitulating to the indignant,

I resonate a mass effect and consummate with my constituent.

Though these words flare, it's not my intention,

I'm asking you believe this fable as I contort the constructs of this dimension.

No need for a red pill, your eyes can magnify past the illusion,

we dwell in relevant anguish while so many squat in comfortable delusion.

Against all temptation we avoid collusion,

all the while staying two inches adjacent to an unforeseen intrusion.

Therapy

You must die…

Wait, maybe it should be me?

It's too easy to blame the voices,

I am…and will always be responsible for my choices.

It occupies the subconscious with an absolute certainty.

I know without just cause…they will murder me.

Do you hear it?

It's the connection due for one so empiric.

Congratulate me or hate me in secret,

there is good in you, hold on to it, keep it!

I'm afraid of what comes next,

give me a way out, let me escape…

There's something magical in the air,

But why does it hide?

It warps the imagination,

but refuses to let me inside!

Don't laugh but I've got a bone to pick,

I'm nowhere near ready but there's damage to inflict.

Was that the strike of a match or did I just suck my teeth?

I'll give you credit, if you peer underneath.

A straight jacket won't hold me and I'm so sick of the aggression,

the second attempt failed, I hope I've learned my lesson.

Thank you for taking this trip with me, I didn't want to do it alone,

but if I can't find happiness here…maybe I'll find it in your home?

Chapter 7

Full Disclosure

全面披露

الكشف الكامل

DIVULGATION COMPLÈTE

ПОЛНОЕ РАСКРЫТИЕ

LA DIVULGACIÓN COMPLETA

Graduation Day

As I stare out at all these young and naïve faces, I shudder to think,

to think the kind of world you believe you're entering and the dreams you'll find extinct.

You are the future but you're also the victim,

and no matter how hard you've studied; extra credit will not grant you wisdom.

You are about to set out on a journey many have taken before you,

many of them are dead, broken or defeated, do not think yourself different, I implore you.

Once you leave these halls you'll face challenges you never thought possible,

you will be hurt, shamed and success in the road ahead will not seem probable.

You will lose more than you've gained and the bottom will be in full view,

you can't come back, you can only push through.

I know this isn't inspirational and not what you expected,

but your next step and "the end" are very much connected.

I am here to tell you that it will be hard and you may fall,

so come ready and give it your all.

Don't expect happiness but don't accept despair,

take hold of what's yours because the person sitting next to you won't care.

Align yourself with those of like minds but stand for yourself,

build internal equity, that's the best type of wealth.

Don't bring a knife to a gunfight and always be ready to fire,

there are those wanting your downfall, so you'll need more than desire.

Live for the moment, rest when you're dead,

take nothing for granted and only the best to your bed.

I wish you the very heights of the potential I see in your eyes,

and remember, no matter how far you fall, never forget to rise!

Tremors

War is inevitable,

defeat is unacceptable,

victory is perceptible,

 this battle will be incredible.

Snitching is on the pedestal,

my victim within my reticle,

his redirect detestable,

tonight will be unforgettable.

The stage already set,

the confession's on cassette,

gotta do what they don't expect,

this is what happens when you slept.

Blind but well fed,

shared but not bread,

Quoted but misread,

slashed to the bone but at least not dead.

Bridging the gap,

less than two seconds, pin hole in the cap.

Breaking their back,

they only gain ground if you slip on attack.

Barking in mockery,

only option is robbery,

opium guiding me,

fore sight in a crimson night, mimicking sodomy!

Victimless progeny,

awakened in misogyny,

he resides where the knowledge be,

wedged against disgrace and distorted apologies.

This is what's inside of me,

heart of lion with skin of a blood-soaked diary.

Close to the end but too far to touch,

fragmented but intact, too determined to need a crutch.

Crawling on hands, three steps from the top,

prostrated, stagnated body ready to drop.

But can't give up, can't surrender,

resilient to fulfillment, until praise is all they could render.

A Letter of Apology

I'm sorry for being there when you needed me,

when the walls closed in close and gave no leniency.

I apologize for making you first and remaining second only to you,

for giving up "me", so "we" could make it through.

I know that it took a lot to be able to step over my corpse after you shattered my soul,

I know my heart was the target; you exceeded intentions and accomplished your goal.

I'm no victim, for I played a part in the end,

whether it was enabling, blind optimism or lack of clarity, I saw the guillotine begin to descend.

But as it approached I stood strong by your side,

the inevitable would always be there but with you, is where I chose to reside.

Now alone in the dark, my actions shine bright,

as I judge my inability to stop my own destruction, it's thoughts of you I hold onto tight.

......isn't that pathetic?

That I could be lying here in ruin, looking at my own failures and not regret it?

How can I lye here in self-pity and not hate you in the least?

Or is it that I'm hiding because the guilt of my inaction would cause all hope to cease?

Is it that I'm so scared of a tomorrow without you I revel in the anguish of your presence?

Am I so lost that I'd rather remain in a constant state of convalescence?

I think I'm done here...

the wound is fresh but my legs can walk and my way is clear.

So yes, I am sorry I won't be around for you to take me for granted,

and when the water gets to be too high, well you might just be stranded.

I apologize that you won't have my constant contact pleading for a piece of your time,

those days are over, the rats can have you, I've accepted you're no longer mine.

I've stayed in this dungeon long enough, I've begged, I've pleaded long enough,

I've given my all and if now you feel empty you can fill that void with my disgust.

I was dying, broken and you were content with my position,

the hurt will pass and I will begin to forget you during the transition.

Your direction, your movement, your place on this Earth is no longer my concern,

we're all connected in this world but it's time to let this connection burn.

We were, what we were for the time we were given,

and now we are none and it's time to begin living...

Mirage

Tell them...

Tell them I had no other choice.

Tell them I loved them more than they knew.

Tell them it wasn't their fault.

Tell them... time will heal the loss.

Tell them I have provided in my absence.

Lie and tell them I was more than this corpse represents.

Lie and tell them I wasn't a coward that lived with nothing but regrets.

Lie and tell them I didn't have my own demons daily haunting my every step.

Lie and tell them it was mortality, not my failures that I couldn't accept.

Lie and tell them I meant something.

Lie and tell them it was an accident... I hadn't planned on jumping.

Make me out to be the person I always hoped to become.

Make me out to be someone of value and importance.

Make me out to be someone you would've felt admiration for, instead of pity.

Make me the friend, lover and companion you would've wanted in your life.

Make me the reflection I never got a chance to see.

Make me a memory worth keeping... something better... anything but me...

12:45am

On the ledge, at the end of my rope,
breaking from the inside, tired of trying to cope.
Beyond hope, too close to harmful temptations,
consumed by futile desires, broken dreams and failed aspirations.

You offered light when all I wanted was dark,
you gave of yourself, you provided a spark.
I thought you were asleep I thought I was alone,
you were there, you were far but stayed with me on the phone.

I looked out and wished I could fly,
I was numb to the world and just wanted to die.
You never left my side, even when I dismissed the pain,
you sat with me while I told you why I couldn't come in from the rain.

I held back tears but still gave me a shoulder without a word,
you didn't judge but allowed me to listen to the agony I never heard.
I should be dead and gone but you didn't give up,
you saw me lost on the street and gave this beggar change for his cup.

More than scribbles or etchings on a page,
a testimony from the forsaken, screaming from his cage.
I thank you for saving me that night,
thank you for not hanging up with when I asked you not to fight.

I lost sight long ago and was content to stagger in insignificance,
with your help, I gained a chance at deliverance.
And although I've slipped, I've stumbled, I've fallen…I'm here,
thank you for giving me another day, when I couldn't contemplate another year.

Forever And A Day

As the autumn beauty blew through the wind, my only thought was…"where is he"?

No response for days; maybe just long hours at work but he'd never been that busy.

I had to know, what if he were hurt or in trouble?

And when all was said and done, all I did was sit here hesitating, mind a jumble.

I grabbed my keys and left,

I drove but by the time I reached my destination I was out of breath.

So intense were my feelings, my hands shaking,

my fear confirmed, seeing his car in the driveway, my spirit breaking.

The grass pristine, the street quiet,

newspapers piled at the door, a sudden chill, unfamiliar to this climate.

I stared up at this modest but charming home and for an instant, I became optimistic,

a vision of a warm welcome combined with a smiling face appeared but I knew wasn't realistic.

The stillness degraded any faded images of promise,

I rang the bell, the lack of reply amongst all other evidence, seemed the strongest.

Hidden in a bed of flowers, the extra key in case of emergency,

I could no longer wait, I felt a great urgency.

I unlocked the door and turned the knob not knowing what lye on the other side,

I opened it slowly, announcing myself to any ears that may reside.

Again, there was no answer to my presence,

the silence felt purposeful, as if some sort of penance.

Night has fallen and in the dark a light peeks out, just past the staircase and down the hall,

I move towards it, hand at my chest, leaning against the wall.

As I rounded the corner, there…at his desk, slumped forward…silent…

I fell to my knees, clutching my stomach, erupting from within me, something violent!

I staggered to my feet and moved closer,

though I wasn't ready, I needed the truth, I needed it to be over.

I pulled him back by the shoulder to find his face covered in blood,

body cold to the touch, a small black gun lying on the rug.

I stepped back, trembling in fear,

I shook my head, trying to make sense out of what should've been so clear.

How did it come to this?

What didn't I see, what did I miss?

Never a negative word spoken,

so far from fragile, he was my rock when I felt broken.

There, in front of him was a note,

I couldn't face his last words, how could I cope?

But maybe within those lines could lie the "why?",

maybe there, he explained why he didn't say goodbye...

To Whom It May Concern,

"If you're reading this, then the pain is at an end,
no longer in hiding, no need to pretend.
I tried my hardest, I did my best,
I stayed as long as I could, it's time to rest.
I know you think me selfish, possibly a coward,
it hurt so much, my courage lie outward.
In you I found strength, with you I could be brave,
alone I felt nothing, alone I saw my grave.

This was my burden, my cross to bear,

I couldn't tell you, it wouldn't have been fair.

The daily inner torment, the scars I can't' forget,

you deserved none of my grief, I only wanted your respect.

This darkness has cost me more than you know and all of who I am,

I moved on in spite, all the while existing as only half a man.

No need for tears, my hourglass was born with a crack,

just live, live the life I couldn't and never look back,

Thank you for loving me but I needed this release,

I'm with you always and now I am at peace."

With Love,

C.F.H.
2/13/22

I thought I knew him, I thought I knew everything,

he was in so much pain, oblivious I went about my life, while he was slowly perishing.

I was in turmoil, trying to decide if we were ever truly friends or was I just an outsider?

Were we as close as I thought or did my ignorance create a divider?

Through it all, he stayed by my side, he meant more than he knew,

in many ways, he was the love of my life, without him...what do I do?

I'm not sure I can leave...

...I don't think I want to...

If he's gone, then there's no place for me,

if he's in a better place, then that's where I want to be.

The weapon, still on the floor,

I knew it was wrong picking it up...knowing the purpose I would use it for.

Like a nightmare I was never destined to awake from,

he's lost and I must find him, with only this one bread crumb.

Before I go, I just needed to explain, I needed you to know why!

I need you to understand, I need you to try.

I know no matter how I start this; the end will burn...

To Whom It May Concern,

....

Just Below Nothing

Through these shadows and dark valley I walk,
an enemy at my back, salvation gone; anguish consumes all thought.
A blind man's vision without prediction,
each step guarded, yet random, lacking precision.

A Captain only in absence of a true leader,
never asking for the role but always too eager.
Fearless with the resolve of a tired soul,
lost but found in his own excrement sipping from an empty bowl.

Two hundred and twenty-eight flashes illuminate a night of grief,
a single barrel, white sheet of paper and one click, hoping to make it brief.
In that moment a decision was made,
a solitary shell remained un-chambered and I'd speak nothing of the life I saved.

One failure after another,
loss after loss with no aspirations to recover.
Enlightened with a closed mind, I saw roses where none bloomed,
I believed I was right and paid the price for what I assumed.

An orphan surrounded by family still praying for an adoption,
stood alone, independent, defiant, progression was the only option.
Considered strange but brilliant, an act for all who would witness,
silently and unsuspectedly though....suffering from Mental Illness.

More secrets now lie just beneath the surface,
the pressure mounting, my own true feelings becoming subversive.
Just a matter of time before I let it go,
then their eyes will be open, then they'll all know.

A friend, one better than I deserve offered me an alternative to the sorrow,
if I took this one step, I could have a different tomorrow.
So I did and the voices became silent,
the anger within, finally became compliant.

Living a dream, I attempted to experience life,
happiness, kids, a home....a wife.
But what held me together began to tear me apart,
I lost my words, my spirit, my essence...that spark!

So I went back to what I knew and where I felt safe,
and in almost an instant it all fell apart and I was left an empty space.
So in the coldest of Novembers I faced a 3rd attempt, instead of a bended knee,
the promising future I imagined was never to be.

Someone once said, "if you can't be there when I'm at my lowest, you don't deserve to be there at my best",
I may never enter the halls of fame but immortality will forever be my guest.
Far from a great man but a man nonetheless,
with each of my failings I gave it my all, I'll let the universe decide the rest.

I still walk in this dark valley with an enemy at my back,
and stumble about in the rags of a king and reside in the humbles of a shack.
I'm a little less than you but far more than where I've been,
a few less secrets confine me, truth now permeates the skin.

Defeat seemed to come easy, it was the smallest victories that were the hardest,
I used to only gauge the misery, now I measure which happy moment I can take the farthest.
I've lived with loss in life but eventually found my purpose and conviction,
it's not the journey I planned for but seeing this road to the end, may finally offer this existence some benediction.

The Next Chapter

This narrative was never mines to tell but it was ours to experience and for that, you have my gratitude.

As the curtain falls, let these last words reverberate in amplitude.

Never let that sensation of hunger leave you or near miss ever equal contentment.

Believe in yourself and forgive missteps, solely upon your spirit become dependent.

Defense in the name of self-preservation is a sovereign distinction,

but don't let an eye for an eye blind us all, until the only achievement is extinction.

Always remember, albeit each of our stories unique, whether fact or fiction,

the truth we are all "one" beneath the surface, may it never fall to attrition.

Let these sentiments contained within be more than inscriptions on a page,

embrace the faults in your reality, the actors have left the stage.

"Frame The Past, Believe In Tomorrow, Exist In The Moment"

www.ingramcontent.com/pod-product-compliance
Lightning Source LLC
LaVergne TN
LVHW091313080426
835510LV00007B/483